ANNE SPENCER
REVISITED

A companion to the film by Keith Lee

Poems by Anne Spencer

Edited and with Notes
by Beth Packert

Photographs of the Anne Spencer House and Garden
by Susan Saandholland

with additional photographs
by Richard C. Burke

and archive materials from the collection of
Nancy Blackwell Marion

BLACKWELL
PRESS
LYNCHBURG, VIRGINIA

ISBN: 978-0-9779523-2-8
Library of Congress Control Number: 2008909671

Published in the United States by Blackwell Press, Lynchburg, Virginia.
Book design by Nancy Blackwell Marion

CONTENTS

4

1975

Turn an earth clod
Peel a shaley rock
In fondness molest a curly worm
Whose *familiar* is everywhere
Kneel
And the curly worm sentient *now*
Will *light* the word that tells the poet what a poem is

Life-Long, Poor Browning . . .

Life-long, poor Browning never knew Virginia,
Or he'd not grieved in Florence for April sallies
Back to English gardens after Euclid's linear:
Clipt yews, Pomander Walks, and pleachéd alleys;

Primroses, prim indeed, in quiet ordered hedges,
Waterways, soberly, sedately enchanneled,
No thin riotous blade even among the sedges,
All the wild country-side tamely impaneled . . .

Dead, now, dear Browning, lives on in heaven,—
(Heaven's Virginia when the year's at its Spring)
He's haunting the byways of wine-aired leaven
And throating the notes of the wildings on wing;

Here canopied reaches of dogwood and hazel,
Beech tree and redbud fine-laced in vines,
Fleet clapping rills by lush fern and basil,
Drain blue hills to lowlands scented with pines . . .

Think you he meets in this tender green sweetness
Shade that was Elizabeth . . . immortal completeness!

Creed

If my garden oak spares one bare ledge
For a boughed mistletoe to grow and wedge;
And all the wild birds this year should know
I cherish their freedom to come and go;
If a battered worthless dog, masterless, alone,
Slinks to my heels, sure of bed and bone;
And the boy just moved in, deigns a glance-assay,
Turns his pockets inside out, calls, "Come and play!"
If I should surprise in the eyes of my friend
That the deed was *my* favor he'd let me lend;
Or hear it repeated from a foe I despise,
That I whom he hated was chary of lies;
If a pilgrim stranger, fainting and poor,
Followed an urge and rapped at my door,
And my husband loves me till death puts apart,
Less as flesh unto flesh, more as heart unto heart:
I may challenge God when we meet That Day,
And He dare not be silent or send me away.

[Dear Langston]

Dear Langston,

    and *that* is what my days
    have brought . . .
    and this: lamp, odorless oil
    round its long
    dried wick:
    Hope without wings
    Love itself contemned
    Where Michael broods,—
    Arc after arc, you see,
    If any where I own
    A circle it is one
    frustrate beginning—

Innocence

She tripped and fell against a star,
A lady we all have known;
Just what the villagers lusted for
To claim her one of their own;
Fallen but once the lower felt she,
So turned her face and died,—
With never a hounding fool to see
'Twas a star-lance in her side!

Epitome

Once the world was young
For I was twenty and very old
And you and I knew all the answers
What the day was, how the hours would turn
One dial was there to see
Now the world is old and I am still young
For the young know nothing, nothing.

Neighbors

Ah, you are cruel;
You ask too much;
Offered a hand, a finger-tip,
You must have a soul to clutch.

Any Wife to Any Husband:
A Derived Poem

This small garden is half my world
I am nothing to it—when all is said,
I plant the thorn and kiss the rose,
But they will grow when I am dead.

Let not this change, Love, the human life
Share with her the joy you had with me,
List with her the plaintive bird you heard with me.
Feel all the human joys, but
Feel most a "shadowy third."

Requiem

Oh, I who so wanted to own some earth,
Am consumed by the earth instead:
Blood into river
Bone into land
The grave restores what finds its bed.

Oh, I who did drink of Spring's fragrant clay,
Give back its wine for other men:
Breath into air
Heart into grass
My heart bereft—I might rest then.

He Said:

"Your garden at dusk
Is the soul of love
Blurred in its beauty
And softly caressing;
I, gently daring
This sweetest confessing,
Say your garden at dusk
Is your soul, My Love."

White Things

Most things are colorful things—the sky, earth, and sea.
　　　　Black men are most men; but the white are free!
White things are rare things; so rare, so rare
They stole from out a silvered world—somewhere.
Finding earth-plains fair plains, save greenly grassed,
They strewed white feathers of cowardice, as they passed;
　　　　　　The golden stars with lances fine,
　　　　　　The hills all red and darkened pine,
They blanched with their wand of power;
And turned the blood in a ruby rose
To a poor white poppy-flower.

They pyred a race of black, black men,
And burned them to ashes white; then,
Laughing, a young one claimed a skull,
For the skull of a black is white, not dull,
　　　　　　But a glistening awful thing;
　　　　　　Made, it seems, for this ghoul to swing
In the face of God with all his might,
And swear by the hell that siréd him:
　　　　　　"Man-maker, make white!"

Dunbar

Ah, how poets sing and die!
Make one song and Heaven takes it;
Have one heart and Beauty breaks it:
Chatterton, Shelley, Keats, and I—
Ah, how poets sing and die!

Lines to a Nasturtium
(A lover muses)

Flame-flower, Day-torch, Mauna Loa,
I saw a daring bee, today, pause, and soar,
    Into your flaming heart;
Then did I hear crisp, crinkled laughter
As the furies after tore him apart?
    A bird, next, small and humming,
Looked into your startled depths and fled. . . .
Surely, some dread sight, and dafter
    Than human eyes as mine can see,
Set the stricken air waves drumming
    In his flight.

Day-torch, Flame-flower, cool-hot Beauty,
I cannot see, I cannot hear your flutey
Voice lure your loving swain,
But I know one other to whom you are in beauty
Born in vain:
Hair like the setting sun,
Her eyes a rising star,
Motions gracious as reeds by Babylon, bar
All your competing;
Hands like, how like, brown lilies sweet,
Cloth of gold were fair enough to touch her feet . . .
Ah, how the sense reels at my repeating,
As once in her fire-lit heart I felt the furies
Beating, beating.

[God never planted a garden]

God never planted a garden
But He placed a keeper there;
And the keeper ever razed the ground
And built a city where
God cannot walk at the eve of day,
Nor take the morning air.

Grapes: Still-Life

Snugly you rest, sweet globes,
Aged essence of the sun;
Copper of the platter
Like that you lie upon.

Is so well your heritage
You need feel no change
From the ringlet of your stem
To this bright rim's flange;

You green-white Niagara,
Cool dull Nordic of your kind,—
Does your thick meat flinch
From these . . . touch and press your rind?

Caco, there, so close to you,
Is the beauty of the vine;
Stamen red and pistil black
Thru the curving line;

Concord, the too peaceful one
Purpling at your side,
All the colors of his flask
Holding high in pride . . .

This, too, is your heritage,
You who force the plight;
Blood and bone you turn to them
For their root is white.

Lady, Lady

Lady, Lady, I saw your face,
Dark as night withholding a star . . .
The chisel fell, or it might have been
You had borne so long the yoke of men.
Lady, Lady, I saw your hands,
Twisted, awry, like crumpled roots,
Bleached poor white in a sudsy tub,
Wrinkled and drawn from your rub-a-dub.
Lady, Lady, I saw your heart,
And altared there in its darksome place
Were the tongues of flames the ancients knew,
Where the good God sits to spangle through.

Po' Little Lib

Half-inch brown spider,
    black-spotted back
Moves thru the grass,
    white-sheeted pack.
M-O-V-E-S thru the grass, O god
if it chance
For the drought driven air turns leaf into lance

Run, escape, wee one you are free . . .
How delicately she re-knits her vast pain
Chance did set her free
What bound her again?

Substitution

Is Life itself but many ways of thought,
How real the tropic storm or lambent breeze
Within the slightest convolution wrought
Our mantled world and men-freighted seas?
God thinks . . . and being comes to ardent things:
The splendor of the day-spent sun, love's birth,—
Or dreams a little, while creation swings
The circle of His mind and Time's full girth . . .
As here within this noisy peopled room
My thought leans forward . . . quick! you're lifted clear
Of brick and frame to moonlit garden bloom,—
Absurdly easy, now, our walking, dear,
Talking, my leaning close to touch your face . . .
His All-Mind bids us keep this sacred place!

For Jim, Easter Eve

If ever a garden was Gethsemane,
with old tombs set high against
the crumpled olive tree—and lichen,
this, my garden, has been to me.
For such as I none other is so sweet:
Lacking old tombs, here stands my grief,
and certainly its ancient tree.

Peace is here and in every season
a quiet beauty.
The sky falling about me
evenly to the compass . . .

What is sorrow but tenderness now
in this earth-close frame of land and sky
falling constantly into horizons
of east and west, north and south;
what is pain but happiness here
amid these green and wordless patterns,—
indefinite texture of blade and leaf:

Beauty of an old, old tree,
last comfort in Gethsemane.

Black Man O' Mine

Black man o' mine,
If the world were your lover,
It could not give what I give to you,
Or the ocean would yield and you could discover
Its ages of treasure to hold and to view;
Could it fill half the measure of my heart's portion . . .
Just for you living, just for you giving all this devotion,
Black man o' mine.

Black man o' mine,
As I hush and caress you, close to my heart,
All your loving is just your needing what's true;
Then with your passing dark comes my darkest part,
For living without your loving is only rue.
Black man o' mine, if the world were your lover
It could not give what I give to you.

ANNE SPENCER IN HER GARDEN

On the Life of Anne Spencer

One day in December 1923, Anne Spencer put on her best red dress, tucked a book of poetry under her arm, and walked the two miles from her house to the Jones Memorial Library—a library that was not open to African-Americans. She walked there because she refused to use the "Jim Crow" trolley system in Lynchburg, Virginia, and she was looking for a job. She carried *The Book of American Negro Poetry*, edited by her friend James Weldon Johnson, to serve as her résumé—it contained five of her poems.

When she got to the library, she had the audacity to propose that when the board of trustees set up a branch library at the local black high school, they should put her in charge of it as librarian. She got what she wanted: the branch library opened at Dunbar High School in January 1924, and Anne Spencer served as its librarian until she retired in 1945. Anne Spencer was a woman who knew what she wanted and how to get it.

She did not want fame, and she cared little for the usual conventions; what she valued were family, friends, and literature. Born in 1882 from a mixture of black, white, and Seminole Indian heritage, Anne Spencer disdained any distinctions based upon race. At the age of eleven, she was sent to a Lynchburg boarding school by parents who set her education as the highest priority; she studied the liberal arts and excelled in languages—Latin, German, and French.

She met Edward Spencer at school, married him in 1901, settled in Lynchburg, and brought up their children, Bethel, Alroy, and Chauncey. Having begun writing poems at school, she continued for her own pleasure, jotting notes and scraps of poetry on bits of paper, old magazines, and even the walls of her house. The Spencers' vibrant intellectual life and colorful house and garden attracted a wide circle of friends.

Anne Spencer came to the attention of the public when James Weldon Johnson, visiting Lynchburg to help start a chapter of the NAACP, stayed with the Spencers. He happened to see one of her poems, which impressed him so powerfully that he helped to get it published. He remained a devoted friend of Anne Spencer's until his death in 1938, and through him she formed relationships with many other important figures, including Langston Hughes, W. E. B. Du Bois, and Paul Robeson, all of whom came to stay with her in Lynchburg. Her poetry was published in journals and anthologies, and she acquired some national prominence as a poet of the Harlem Renaissance in the 1920s.

After Johnson's death, she continued to write poetry, but she did not seek publication. She and Edward cultivated their garden and provided a lively social life for their family and friends. They were influential in the civil rights movement and encouraged their son, Chauncey, to fly to Washington, D.C., in 1939 to persuade Congress to fund the Tuskegee Airmen. Edward died in 1964; Anne was bereft, but she went on writing poems and working in her garden. She died in 1975.

On Anne Spencer's House and Garden

When Anne and Edward Spencer married in 1901, they settled in Lynchburg, Virginia, where Edward had a big family—he was one of eleven children. The Spencer family owned a large amount of land, including a former Confederate Army campground, Camp Davis, where the family had once given lodging to freed slaves. Edward Spencer operated Spencer Place, a private residential development, as well as a family grocery store, and in 1903, just down the street from the store, he built the house at 1313 Pierce Street where he and Anne lived the rest of their lives. Many other Spencers lived nearby, and Anne and Edward's house became a gathering spot for family and friends.

Any visitor can see immediately why the Spencers' house captivated guests, including many famous and well-traveled people. The house was unusual for its time; Edward installed central heat and a modern bathroom before such conveniences were common in Lynchburg, and Anne's love of bold colors is apparent in the striking greens, blues, reds, and purples used on the walls and in the furnishings. Anne had a telephone booth built under the stairs so that she could enjoy private conversations—her notes are still visible on the walls. To improve the house, Edward cleverly employed materials he discovered as he walked the city streets delivering parcels for the post office. A large mirror, discarded from a mansion undergoing renewal, was restored and placed in the living room. Copper panels from a store display became wainscoting in the dining room. When they needed an extra shelf, Edward made one with a picture frame and some hooks. Friends also helped to decorate the house. Amaza Lee Meredith, a well-known black architect and art professor, made a tiled mantelpiece that commemorates the poem "Lines to a Nasturtium" (about Anne Spencer's favorite flower), while a granddaughter, Dolly Allen Mason, painted a mural of a cocktail party in the upstairs bedroom because

Edward decided it was time to discourage Anne's habit of writing on the wall when she had an inspiration in the middle of the night.

The Spencers extended their innovations into the garden, starting with a small plot near the house, then expanding it into several garden rooms over two lots, all the way back to Buchanan Street. In 1924, Edward built a garden cottage for Anne that they called Edankraal (the name combined Ed, Anne, and the Afrikaans word for dwelling). They added a pergola for wisteria, a grape arbor, and piping to carry water to a pool with fish and water lilies. They laid paths, put up a fence (using fancy iron work discarded by Randolph-Macon Woman's College), and erected bird houses on poles so tall they needed the fire department's help to install them. W. E. B. Du Bois brought Anne an African bust from the Ebo (Igbo) tribe, and they turned it into a fountain they named Prince Ebo. The garden was lovingly maintained by both Anne and Edward (they had help to cook and clean, but they did all the gardening themselves), and it provided a center of tranquility for them and their friends, as well as a source of inspiration for much of Anne's poetry.

The house is preserved with the original furnishings and appears much as it was when Anne Spencer was alive. The garden has been carefully restored by the Hillside Garden Club under the direction of Jane B. White. Both are open to visitors.

On the Composition of the Poems

When James Weldon Johnson met Anne Spencer in 1918, he discovered a woman who shared his passions for reading and writing, and they remained the closest of friends until his death in 1938. Johnson was immediately impressed by the skillfulness of her poems, and he made certain that her work became known in literary circles far from Lynchburg.

Spencer was still in school when she wrote her first poem, now lost, a sonnet called "Skeptic." In spite of the demands of her family and household, and the perennial pull of her garden, she wrote constantly, all her life. Her papers are full of scraps of poems and notes written on every available surface, including envelopes, garden catalogs, and the margins of magazines. Not even the walls of her house escaped her constant urges to write, and finally Edward tried to thwart her late-night scribbles by installing wood paneling in their bedroom (along with their granddaughter's mural). Spencer also was a voracious reader, and her poems often allude to favorite writers such as Robert Browning, John Keats, Paul Laurence Dunbar, and Ralph Waldo Emerson. Several poems refer to family and friends: "Lady, Lady" is about the Spencers' laundress; "Black Man O' Mine" is addressed to Edward Spencer.

Johnson sent Spencer's work to the critic H. L. Mencken, who wrote back approving it, and her first published poem appeared in the NAACP journal, *The Crisis*, in 1920. With the encouragement of Johnson and other friends, such as Langston Hughes, she published poems regularly until 1931, and her work was included in a number of anthologies and collections. Her last new published poem, "For Jim, Easter Eve," written after James Weldon Johnson's death, appeared in an anthology edited by Langston Hughes in 1949. Although she wrote poetry all the rest of her life, she did not continue to seek publication. Poetry was, for her, a more private pleasure. Spencer explained to her biographer Lee Greene that, to make a poem, she would start "with a word or two and begin associating." She would sometimes have the germ of an idea for years before she actually wrote a poem. Spencer revised her poems many times, refining them even after they were published. Her sonnet "Substitution," published in 1927, was last revised in 1973.

Several of the poems focus on the theme of death, including "Requiem," first published in 1931. "Life-Long, Poor Browning . . ." is a response to Robert Browning's poem "Home-Thoughts from Abroad." Browning's poem "Any Wife to Any Husband" inspired Spencer's poem of the same name. Both of Spencer's poems use the garden to explore the meaning of death and the loss of a loved one.

Other poems address social issues. "Creed" was written after Anne took a trip with Edward to the site of John Brown's rebellion at Harper's Ferry, West Virginia, where she noticed an oak tree covered with mistletoe. She also began writing a five-canto poem called "A Dream of John Brown: On His Return Trip Home," which she never finished. Spencer wrote "Innocence" in response to the community gossip about a young woman's pregnancy. Similarly, "Neighbors" reflects Spencer's impatience with the scandal caused by her disregard for convention, such as when she wore a pantsuit to a picnic or hopped on the back of a grocery wagon instead of riding the trolley. Her angriest poem, published first in 1923, is "White Things," which she wrote after reading a description of a pregnant black woman killed when a lynch mob cut open her abdomen. In contrast, "Grapes: Still-Life" addresses racism more indirectly and metaphorically.

Most of the poems illuminate Spencer's view of her world and herself. According to Lee Greene, "Epitome" was prompted by Edward's comments to his girls, who wanted to do something their mother opposed; Edward said, "Your mother was never young." When the children had questions, he said, "Ask your mother; she will tell you whether she knows or not." The poem "He Said" is a testament to Edward's devotion to Anne and the garden they tended together. Spencer's correspondence with poet Langston Hughes inspired "Dear Langston," a poem from her notebooks. Her last completed poem, "1975," was actually written in June 1974. She chose the title in accord with her expectation that she would die in 1975. The poem illustrates her attachment to her garden, her deepest source of inspiration.

On the Making of *Anne Spencer Revisited,* a film by Keith Lee

Keith Lee has been an artist most of his life. Born in the Bronx, New York, Lee trained as a dancer and then performed with American Ballet Theatre. He began choreographing ballets for many companies and taught dance at several schools, including the Alvin Ailey American Dance Theater. In 1999, Lee helped to found Dance Theatre of Lynchburg, and he is well known in the community for his work with young dancers.

Like many residents of Lynchburg, Lee had heard of the Anne Spencer House and Garden for years before he actually paid a visit there. When he finally came to the house and garden, they entranced him, and Lee knew he wanted to create a tribute to Anne Spencer and her legacy. In considering how to make such a tribute, Lee finally decided to venture in a new direction—he determined to make a film. Nina Salmon, a Lynchburg College English

KEITH LEE, SUSAN SAANDHOLLAND, AND SONIA LANGHORNE

professor and Anne Spencer specialist, gave him advice and historical background. He obtained permission to film at the Anne Spencer House and Garden Museum in October and November of 2007.

After a search for the best person to portray Anne Spencer, Lee discovered Sonia Langhorne, a young actor who also writes poetry. To portray Anne Spencer as a girl, Lee decided to use his own daughter Eliana Inez Lee. Also joining the project was Phil Spinner, a local filmmaker with Heritage Media Services, who took charge of lighting, filming, and editing, with the help of Melanie Elliotte. Barbara Webb agreed to assist with costuming.

Lee also asked Susan Saandholland to participate in the project. A freelance photographer with a studio at Riverviews Artspace in Lynchburg, Saandholland had previously worked with Lee on a book of dance photographs, *On the Threshold of the Dream*. Saandholland would produce photographic stills of Langhorne, the house, and the garden that would become part of the finished film.

Having assembled his personnel, Lee began making the film. Langhorne memorized several of Spencer's poems and performed them in costume in a series of twelve vignettes at the Anne Spencer House and Garden. Filming was completed by mid-January 2008, and the film was edited with the addition of Saandholland's stills. In April and May 2008, the film was shown to enthusiastic audiences in and around Lynchburg.

ANNE AND EDWARD SPENCER

A Note of Thanks

This project was made possible by the generous support of the Virginia Foundation for the Humanities and the following people: Virginia P. Packert, Hugh J. M. Jones, III, Bonnie Packert, Fred Watkins, and Nancy Blackwell Marion.

The following people kindly provided advice and assistance: Richard C. Burke (who also took the photograph on page 8 and the house interior shots), Nina V. Salmon, Sandra L. Wilson, and Mrs. Chauncey E. Spencer, Sr. Additional thanks go to Keith Lee for his advice on the book and the use of his title, and to Susan Saandholland for her assistance in the book design.

This project was made possible by the Virginia Foundation for the Humanities. The Virginia Foundation for the Humanities was established in 1974 to develop and support public programs, education, and research in the humanities and to relate the humanities to public issues. The VFH promotes understanding and use of the humanities through public debate, group discussion, and individual inquiry. Principal activities of the Virginia Foundation include an internationally recognized Fellowship Program, the Virginia Folklife Program, the Virginia Center for Media and Culture, a statewide network of Regional Councils, and the Grant Program. The VFH is non-profit and non-partisan and receives support from private gifts, grants and contributions, and from the National Endowment for the Humanities and the Commonwealth of Virginia. For more information, write or call the Foundation's office at 145 Ednam Drive, Charlottesville, Virginia 22903-4629, (434) 924-3296, or visit the VFH online at www.virginiafoundation.org.

The project is presented as a public service. The principal aim of the project is to discuss in an objective and nonpartisan context issues of concern and interest to citizens of the Commonwealth of Virginia. The views and opinions expressed in this project do not necessarily represent those of the Virginia Foundation, its contributors, or its supporting agencies.

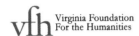

Sources and Further Reading

The following sources provided essential information in the preparation of this book and should be consulted by readers who wish to study additional poems or more historical details. The best source on Anne Spencer's life is *Time's Unfading Garden: Anne Spencer's Life and Poetry*, by J. Lee Greene (Baton Rouge: Louisiana State University Press, 1977). The definitive study of the garden is *Half My World: The Garden of Anne Spencer, a History and Guide*, by Rebecca T. Frischkorn and Reuben M. Rainey (Lynchburg, VA: Warwick House, 2003). A useful shorter work is *Anne Spencer: "Ah, how poets sing and die!"* by Nina V. Salmon (Lynchburg, VA: Warwick House, 2001).

"COCKTAIL PARTY" MURAL BY DOLLY ALLEN MASON